The Marriage Builders' Seminar Handbook

A Marriage Enrichment Advance
Helping to Build the Foundation of Marriage

Couple's Manuel

Compiled by Steven R. Cain

[Type here]

DEDICATION

To all the married couples who have planted and sowed their marriage with the Word of God

SESSIONS

ACKNOWLEDGMENTS

To all the people who will make the Marriage Seminar a success in the coming years. To those who will dedicate their live to fulfill the mission that God has given to them. To those who stand firm.

Ephesians 6:13-20 (*English Standard Version*)

[13] Therefore take up the whole armor of God, that you may be able to withstand in the evil day, and having done all, to stand firm.

[14] Stand therefore, having fastened on the belt of truth, and having put on the breastplate of righteousness,

[15] and, as shoes for your feet, having put on the readiness given by the gospel of peace.

[16] In all circumstances take up the shield of faith, with which you can extinguish all the flaming darts of the evil one;

[17] and take the helmet of salvation, and the sword of the Spirit, which is the word of God,

[18] praying at all times in the Spirit, with all prayer and supplication. To that end keep alert with all perseverance, making supplication for all the saints,

[19] and also for me, that words may be given to me in opening my mouth boldly to proclaim the mystery of the gospel,

[20] for which I am an ambassador in chains, that I may declare it boldly, as I ought to speak.

HELPING TO BUILD THE FOUNDATION OF MARRIAGE

Thank you for attending the Marriage Builders' Seminar. We hope that you have settled in for a weekend of fellowship, growing together and the study of the Word of God. The Marriage Builders' Seminar was put together so that couples could draw closer together by learning what the Word of God tells them about marriage.

From the time of Adam and Eve, the first couple, God has placed a husband and wife together to create an institution of marriage between a man and a woman. We must forge ahead with the Word of God to help keep this sacred institution together. That is why we have developed the Marriage Builders' Seminar.

Marriage in the world today has gone haywire. The world has put its two-cents in and is trying to destroy the sacredness of this, which was established by God. In this weekend seminar, you will learn what it means to have a marriage built on His Word. You will learn how a man thinks, how a woman thinks. Then you will see how it all comes together by laying the foundation for a Godly marriage.

So, we start this seminar by letting you know that you are building your marriage on the true Word of God.

SESSION 1 - IN THE BEGINNING

Before you attend each session, we would like for you to read in the Marriage Builders Handbook the corresponding chapters. This workbook is to help you take and record notes during the entire seminar.

As we start out on this journey in building our marriage on God's truths, we want to do like anyone else would do and that's start at the beginning.

Genesis 3:1 _____

_____

_____

A Few things that Satan Lies to Eve about

1. God is keeping something from you. _____

_____

_____

2. You will receive a benefit if you sin. _____

_____

_____

3. You will be more like God. _____

_____

4. You will be more intelligent and have more understanding. _____

_____

Sin has its Fruit.

_____

_____

_____

_____

_____

_____

Session 2 - Trust + Time =Love

Time and love. Those two words seem like they go hand in hand. Today, love is everywhere we look. Love is on the greeting cards we receive. Love is in the movies (though it can be the wrong type). Love is on TV; Love is in magazines and on the newsstands. But to love and trust is a whole different thing.

10 Key Elements in Building Trust

1. Tell the truth. _____

_____

_____

2. Be where you are supposed to be. _____

_____

_____

3. Be a good steward. _____

_____

_____

4. Communicate: leave a note/call on the phone. _____

_____

_____

5. Be on time. _____

_____

_____

6. Be obedient. _____

_____

_____

7. Do a good job. _____

_____

_____

8. Make things important. _____

_____

_____

9. Be grateful. _____

_____

_____

10. Have a good attitude. _____

_____

_____

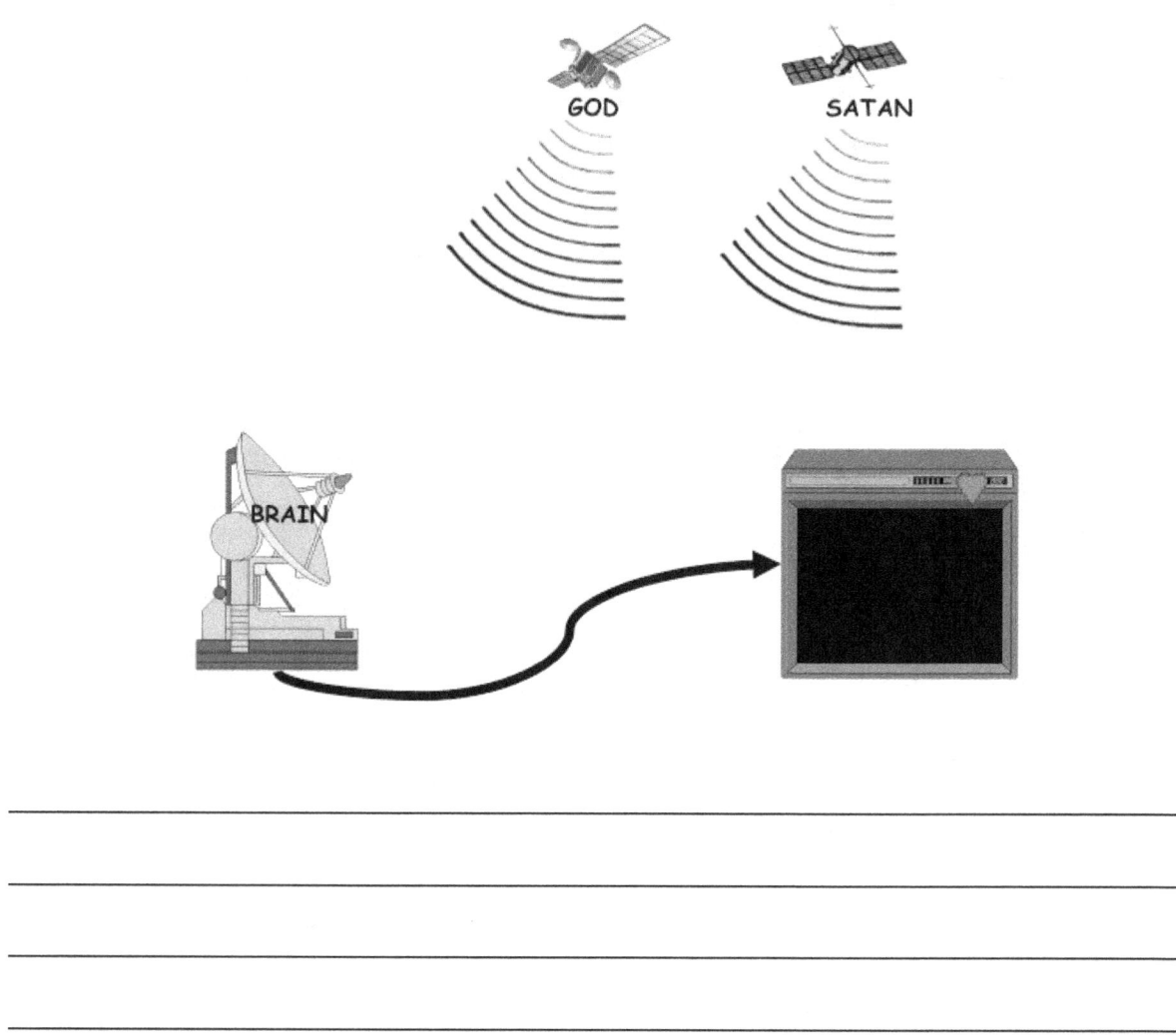

_____

_____

_____

_____

Psalm 119:9 says, "Wherewithal shall a young man cleanse his way? by taking heed thereto according to thy word."

Psalm 119:10 says, "With my whole heart have I sought thee: O let me not wander from thy commandments." Psalm 119:11 says, "Thy word have I hid in mine heart, that I might not sin against thee." Or in other words "that I might not choose the wrong channel."

_____

_____

Session 3 - Expectations

Expectations are coupled with rights. How many of you know that you have different expectations than your spouse has? I ask young couples in pre-martial counseling if they have shared with their mate their expectations of marriage. Often, they have never thought about that. We all have our expectations. You wouldn't get married if you didn't expect to spend the rest of your life together. The reality is that many couples do not spend the rest of their lives together, because of unmet expectations.

What types of expectations do you expect from your mate? _____

_____

_____

Judas as an illustration _____

_____

_____

Do you have any bitterness toward your spouse? If so, what? _____

_____

_____

Joseph, the star witness _____

_____

_____

_____

Honor Chart

Christ   **Honor**

Dad   **Responsibility**

             Authority

Mom   **Helpmate**

Youth   **Learning**

Session 4 – Honor, Part One

What is honor? _____

_____

What happened in Old Testament marriages? _____

_____

_____

Who is the boss? _____

_____

Consist -_____

_____

Honor -_____

_____

_____

Honor, Part Two

Where do we learn honor? _____

_____

_____

One foundation for building an intimate relationship is trust. Another is _____

_____

Are we commanded to be kind? _____

_____

_____

Session 5 - Knowledge of Good and Evil

In the book of Genesis, we see something that the early church had taught through the ages that we have lost. Let's look at Genesis to lay the ground work of why the teaching is so important. Then we will look at the application and how it will affect your life.

_____

_____

_____

_____

The garden where God created Adam and Eve was where marriage started and until the serpent came, Adam and Eve had complete fellowship with Holy God.

_____

_____

_____

_____

_____

_____

What is Satan's nature? _____

_____

_____

_____

Who is your final authority? _____

_____

_____

_____

Explain the two sets of good and evil. _____

_____

_____

_____

_____

_____

_____

Everyone who reads this book or have been in church long enough knows that when Jesus died on the cross He shed His blood as the Lamb of God to take away the sins of the world. What can wash away my sins? Nothing but the Blood. What can make me whole again? Nothing but the Blood!

Session 6 - Root Causes of Conflict

How many of you have ever had an argument in your marriage? To resolve it, did you deal with the root or the fruit? Most people deal with the fruit of the argument. You can trace almost every argument to five or six things. The number one thing is your expectations. I have news for you. If your church does not live up to your expectations, what would you do? Do you know the number one reason that people leave the church? They expect everything to run smoothly without any problems. They think everyone is going to love them and no one will ever say anything to hurt their feelings.

_____

_____

_____

One cause of conflict is the assumption of **rights**.

_____

_____

_____

How about **blame**? Have you ever blamed someone? You think your wife caused you to eat that fruit of the tree of Good and Evil. _It's my wife's fault_, you think. Will the Lord stand for that?

_____

_____

_____

How about **guilt**? Did you know that guilt can cause conflicts? _____

_____

_____

_____

Pride is another cause of conflict. How many think they have a problem with pride? I will not ask you, because you can be prideful and not know it! But I could find out from your spouse!

_____

_____

_____

Lust causes conflict when our selfishness supersedes our love for others.

_____

_____

_____

All the root causes of conflict we just discussed are also causes of war. War comes because of rights being challenged.

War Comes Because...

- **Our rights are challenged**
- **Our expectations are not met**
- **Our pride is in the way (even Paul had to deal with pride)**
- **Guilt causes us to strike out**
- **We try to defend ourselves and blame others**
- **We or someone we love is hurt**
- **We are selfish**

Chapter 7 - Learning Center of the Man

The learning center of a man's mind is different from a woman's mind. Women are reactionary. A man's mind is like an office building, like high rise buildings with lights in the windows.

A MAN MAY GO INTO MANY DIFFERENT OFFICES THAT HE MUST THINK ABOUT. HE SEES THE DETAILS THAT NEED TO BE DONE AND THINKS ON THEM.

_____

_____

_____

_____

_____

_____

Writing a note for a man will help him get things done, and help him to remember what he needs to do. Men often need these little tidbits of information to make progress. Men have a hard time remembering what the wife has said for him to do.

_____

_____

_____

_____

SO, LADIES, GIVE HIM INFORMATION IN A BRIEF MEMO SO HE REMEMBERS WHAT TO DO WITHOUT <u>CONSTANT</u> VERBAL REMINDERS.

_____

_____

_____

_____

Ladies, if you can write it down and it will get it off your mind. Men if your wife gives you a memo and you throw it away; your wife will take that as rejection. She will think that she is not very important to you. She will not believe that you cherish her. She will not think you want her around. Those things are important to her, and she wants to include you in her world.

Let's continue looking at the male mind. In one way, it is like a microscope.

_____

_____

_____

_____

_____

For example, how many wives encourage husbands to stop for directions? He doesn't want to do it, because he knows where he is going. Even though he has put it on his microscope and examined it from every angle, he still can make a mistake.

_____

_____

_____

_____

Men, you do not realize that just because you have been at work all day you have the right to come home and just be a clam. If your wife does not talk to you, and confide in you about her life, that puts her into temptation to talk to someone **else.**

_____

_____

_____

_____

_____

Sometimes a person is not able to forgive others because they have not come to the Savior and asked the Lord Jesus Christ to forgive them of their sins. Once you have been forgiven yourself, you will want to forgive others. If you have a problem with forgiveness, I suggest you go back through the Gospel message. Talk to someone who can explain it well and make sure that you have received the forgiveness of all your sins.

Session 8 - The Auditorium of a Woman's Mind

A woman's mind is like a large auditorium.

_____

_____

_____

You can also picture a woman's mind with a rug in it.

_____

_____

_____

_____

_____

_____

A woman's mind is also like radar.

_____

_____

_____

_____

_____

_____

_____

When men come home from work, they rest. However, a woman's work is never done. When men come home from work, they do not want to think about work or the day's happenings. But women are different. Women are very descriptive, and men want just the facts. She wants to talk about her day the minute he gets home.

You are supposed to minister to your wife. Listen with undivided attention and understanding when she talks.

Session 9 - Communication

As we come to the subject of marriage communication it is one of the most vital parts.

What is a rule of marriage? _____

_____

_____

Consist means _____

_____

What is marriage? _____

_____

MY PROMISE...

HEAVENLY FATHER'S PROMISE...

Covenant

Marriage is a covenant; it's not a contract It is a covenant.

_____

_____

_____

Marriage can work through the five senses.

_____

_____

_____

In marriage there must be communication, and even though two people merge, and they become one flesh, they still need to communicate to each other as two individuals.

_____

_____

_____

_____

Let's first talk about the communication with the soul. The soul is made up of the mind which is knowledge, emotions which are feelings, and the will, which is choices that we make. in your relationship, you will gain more knowledge about each other. And with that knowledge you'll experience feelings. When you have a good marriage and you talk things over, you share your feelings. Then the will makes choices, and sometimes these choices is where a conflict comes, but if we really want to serve each other, and we really want to build a strong relationship, we can talk about those choices, with the right attitude honoring and loving one another.

_____

_____

_____
_____
_____

SPIRIT _____

_____

_____

Never allow things in your life to cause you to withdraw your spirit or your desire from your husband or your wife. One of the ways that you do that is in your own life make sure that you never do or say anything that causes your mate to be ungrateful, and to have a bad attitude towards you. Look for those things that you are <u>thankful</u> for in your mate.

_____

_____

_____

By keeping the desire and spiritual bond together, you'll find that your communication will be better. You will find you'll feel better, which affects your soul: mind, will, and emotions. Most of all you will find it affects your physical body, and that relationship!

_____

_____

_____

It's important to not let anyone <u>distract</u> you from the importance of your marriage, and keeping your desires towards your mate. I know you love your children, but don't put them ahead of your marriage. I know that you have friends, but don't put them ahead of your marriage. I know that you have an occupation, but don't make that more important than your marriage. Don't make any other relationship that you build more important than your mate. Keep in mind that one day the children will grow up, and they'll be gone. There will be you and your mate, if you will grow together and honor and cherish one another in the previous years.

_____

_____

_____

_____

The spotlight of God's grace...

_____

_____

_____

_____

_____

Don't live in the past.

_____

_____

_____

I know that you want to make wise choices, so stay in the spotlight, stay in the now.

_____

_____

_____

_____

Session 10 - Rights and Responsibilities

In the last few years there has been a campaign to teach women, children, adults and seniors their rights. But you don't hear about people talking about responsibilities, do you?

_____

_____

_____

_____

So, if you focus on your rights without your responsibilities you are building up rebellion in your heart. As people get in fusses and fights, it is always about their rights (one of the major causes).

_____

_____

_____

_____

How many of your know that we have the freedom of speech in America? I tell you a lot of people major on this. "I have a right to say whatever I want!" Is that right? That is what the world thinks. Freedom of Speech! What is our responsibility? In James 1:26 it says, "If any man among you seems to be religious and bridles not his tongue, but deceives his own heart, this man's religion is vain." Does the Word of God balance our rights with our responsibilities? I hope that when you read the Word of God that you will learn to balance your rights with your responsibilities.

_____

_____

_____

_____

_____

A matter of fact, Christianity says that you are to die to self. "To be crucified with Christ (Gal. 2:20)," remember? How many rights do you have? Some men say, "I have a right to have dinner on the table at 6:00 o'clock every night." Some women say, "I have a right to go out Friday night by myself if I want to." You don't realize how many rights that you have accumulated in your mind, until you have it exposed!

_____

_____

_____

_____

Did Christ trust us with the Gospel? Do you realize that you are the best that he has here? Did you know that He has trusted you with the Holy Spirit? He has trusted you with the Word of God, and we are to have a good relationships that others see. But if you focus on your rights without your responsibilities, you will have argument after argument. In Acts 20:35 it says, "I have shown you all things how so laboring that you are to support the weak to remember the words of the Lord Jesus how He said, 'it is more blessed to give than to receive.'"

_____

_____

_____

_____

Session 11 - Types of Guilt

Godly guilt is not a type of punishment. It is like the fire alarm in your house. If there is smoke or fire it will go off. In marriage when people feel guilty it causes a break in communication. If you sense Godly guilt it means God is trying to tell you something. The second type of guilt is from Satan, and the third type is called false guilt. We need to identify these three types of guilt, because when you know the source, you know how to deal with it.

Godly guilt - James 2:10 says, "For whosoever shall keep the whole law, and yet offend in one *point*, his is guilty of all."

THIS VERSE SAYS WHEN YOU BREAK GOD'S LAWS YOU WILL FEEL GUILTY.

_____

_____

_____

_____

_____

WHEN WE DO SOMETHING THAT IS AGAINST WHAT GOD HAS COMMANDED US TO DO WE HAVE THE SENSE WITHIN OURSELVES THAT CAUSES US TO FEEL EMBARRASSED OR JUST PLAIN GUILTY BECAUSE WE HAVE OFFENDED GOD.

_____

_____

_____

_____

TRUE GUILT IS GOOD, BECAUSE IT MEANS THAT GOD IS TALKING TO YOU—THAT IS A BLESSING.

_____

_____

_____

It is a perfect love that no one here one earth can give to us.

GODLY GUILT IS GIVEN FOR GETTING US TO **CHANGE** OUR DIRECTION. WHY IS THIS IMPORTANT?

_____

_____

_____

_____

_____

_____

_____

_____

Once we have changed our direction and have confessed our sins then true Godly guilt leaves.

Satanic Guilt - "Then Satan answered the LORD, and said, Doth Job fear for nought?" -Job 1:9-11

Satanic guilt comes from Satan. You won't find too many verses on this, but Rev. 12:10 says this "And I heard a loud voice saying in heaven, now is come salvation, and strength, and the kingdom of our God, and the power of his Christ: for the **accuser of our brethren** is cast down, which accused them before our God day and night."

_____

_____

_____

_____

Satanic guilt will cause you to absorb the wrong-doing.

_____

_____

_____

_____

Satanic guilt is real, and if you believe Satan, he will torment you and rob you of the joy of your salvation.

_____

_____

_____

_____

Satanic guilt is real. When you become, a born-again Christian Satan does not want you to witness, he does not want you to serve the Lord or to worship the Lord. He does not want you to love your neighbor or have unity in the church. Satan continually tries to get people to accuse one another, and when one suffers in the church, the whole church suffers. Be careful.

Satan uses extreme guilt to torment the person, and they end up not forgiving themselves.

_____

_____

_____

_____

False Guilt - "And they watched him, whether he would heal him on the Sabbath day: that **they might accuse him."**— Mark 3:2

_____

_____

_____

_____

A good illustration of false guilt is that of the Pharisees. Remember that Jesus just fed the five thousand, performed miracles, and on the Sabbath, He healed a person. The religious leaders saw Him healing this person on the Sabbath day, and they were ready to excite the people and to stone Him for breaking the Sabbath.

What did He do? He said in Mark 12:11-12, "What man shall there be among you, that shall have one sheep, and if it falls into a pit on the Sabbath day, will he not lay hold on it, and lift it out?" They agreed. Then He asked, "How much then is a man better than a sheep?" That is where the Word of God comes to the rescue. The Pharisees taught the letter of the Law, but Jesus taught the heart of the law.

_____

_____

_____

_____

False guilt comes from man. I John 1:9 says that if we confess our sins He is faithful and just to forgive us. Christ not only forgives us but cleanses us from all unrighteousness.

What happens if you truly confess your sin and ask for forgiveness, but the thought of that sin comes back again? That is not Godly guilt – it's Satanic guilt.

_____

_____

_____

Occasionally you can forget if you asked for forgiveness of a sin.

_____

_____

People like to remind you of your sins. Don't let your past sins keep you down

_____

_____

We need each other. We need to minister to one another, meet each other's needs and grow together.

Session 12 - Walking in the Spirit

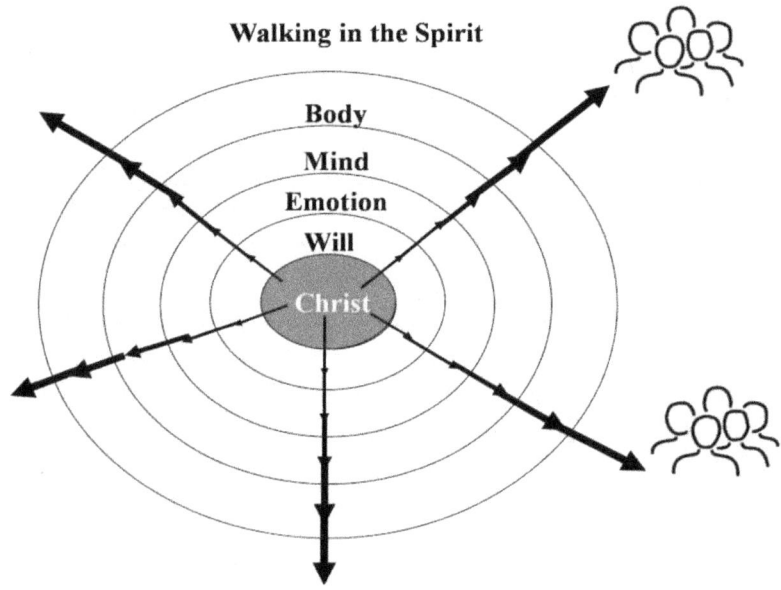

How do you live the Christian life? Most people think that you live the Christian life by disciplining the body. "I am not going to let my body do what it used to do."

"But you are not in the flesh, but in the Spirit if so be that the Spirit of God dwell in you. Now if any man has not the Spirit of Christ, he is none of His. But if the Spirit of Him that rose Jesus from the dead dwells in you, He that rose Christ from the dead shall also quicken your mortal bodies by His Spirit that dwells in you." (Romans 8:9-11).

_____

_____

So, you become a Christian and Christ is in the center. All the Holy Spirit you need for all eternity is inside of you. The power of God is inside of you. His holiness is inside of you.

_____

To let the Holy Spirit, use you, you must let Him freely into your life. You must surrender your will to Him to for Him to use you.

_____

_____

Emotions

The main thing is that you give your emotions to the Lord.

_____

_____

Emotions are a good thing. God gave us emotions to help us out in our normal way of life. So, don't be afraid to show emotions when God's Holy Sprit moves upon you. For some of us it is a great relief to have these emotions.

_____

_____

Mind/Body

So, we are going to surrender our will, emotions, and mind so that the Holy Spirit comes through. Then what happens to the body? Then the body gets filled with the Holy Spirit. And before you know it, the Holy Spirit that lives inside is touching other people!

_____

_____

_____

"And walk in the Spirit and you will not fulfill the lust of the flesh." (Galatians 5:16). "If we live in the Spirit, let us also walk in the Spirit. (Galatians 5:25).

_____

_____

_____

Now you will understand James 2:20 that people have a hard time understanding. They wonder, "If you are saved by grace why does James say, 'But wilt thou know vain man, that faith without works is dead?'" If you have faith, you will have works, because when you are filled with the Holy Spirit things are going to change!

_____

_____

_____

Now, what happens when the Christian sins? Sin comes in the body, that will affect the mind, then affect your emotions and choices, and where is the Holy Spirit? Deep inside.

_____

_____

_____

Is there any reason for us not to be "walking in the Spirit?" Hasn't the Lord made every provision, so we can?

_____

_____

_____

Are you willing to give up being the final authority in your life? Because that is where it all starts. "Lord, not my will, but thine will be done." (Luke 22:42).

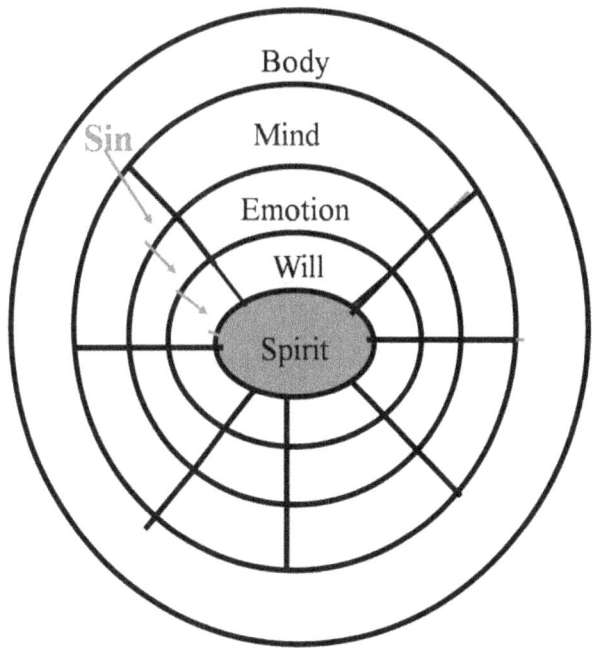

Session 13 - Fear

Our Nation is in fear; a lot of people have different kinds of fear, and they fear different things, but I think that it is very important that we have a sound mind. I think it very important that we trust God in what He says in the things that we face every day. You know some people approach the Bible as a history book, but the Word of God was given to us to apply to our lives today. His Word is just as powerful today as it was back in the Old Testament, in the days of Christ, in the early church. So, we must have faith and faith destroys fear. Also fear destroys faith. Unbelief is fear in disguise.

_____

_____

_____

_____

Oswald Chambers speaks of the two different kinds of fear, and he says this, " The remarkable thing about fearing God is that when you fear God, you fear nothing else, whereas if you do not fear God, you fear everything else". You see, as Christians we need to be available to do whatever God wants us to do. We do not have to fix it all. But whatever comes in your life, He will never leave you or forsake you. He is there with you, and He will see you through it whatever it is.

_____

_____

_____

_____

But fear causes you to do strange things, and fear is real, and we need to know how to deal with it. We know that when the disciples were on the water in the boat, and Jesus came walking on that water, we find that the disciples thought that it was a spirit. In Matthew 14: 22 it says, "That when His disciples saw Him walking on the sea they were troubled saying it is a spirit and they cried out for fear". These were the men that walked and talked and ate with Jesus, and they were afraid! What about in verse 27? It says, "But straightway Jesus spake unto them saying be of good cheer it is I. Be not afraid."

_____

_____

_____

_____

You see as Christians we need to be available to do whatever God wants us to do. We do not have to fix it all. But whatever comes in your life, He will never leave you or forsake you. He is there with you, and He will see you through it.

_____

_____

_____

_____

In Matt. 14: 30 you remember Peter walked on the water, but when he felt the water underneath his feet and the wind, and when he saw those huge waves he got afraid didn't he? Guess what happened? He started to sink.

_____

_____

_____

_____

How to destroy fear is to build your faith. How do you build your faith?

_____

_____

_____

_____

Sometimes when trying to get couples back together again, they have a fear that if they get back together that the same thing is going to happen again. I see people staying in the wilderness for forty years trying to work it out. I know other's that trust the Lord and work it out immediately.

_____

_____

_____

_____

Sometimes, I like to say, 'Why do you want to stay in the wilderness? Why not trust the Lord in what He says and go into the Promised Land of peace and happiness and love?" There are those who don't get together because they are afraid of how they are going to feel the rest of their lives. Fear keeps people from finding the Promised Land. Fear keeps people from having a sound mind. Fear keeps people from having the relationships that God wants them to have daily. The Israelites disobeyed God. So, the result of it was that no one went into the Promised Land.

_____

_____

_____

_____

He had to raise a new generation that had been fed in the wilderness, had seen God do mighty acts, and had the pillar of fire by night and cloud by day.

_____

_____

_____

_____

What kept the nation of Israel, the army of Israel from fighting Goliath? They were afraid.

So, God has a sense of humor, He raised up a teenager. Someone that was no politician, no one of any importance to the world; he was merely a shepherd, and he believed the Word of God. He said that these Philistines have blasphemed the Highest God, and that they are living dangerously. He took what he had, a slingshot and some rocks, and he went in and slew Goliath. My friend, God will take what you have in your hand and slay all your fears, if you will trust Him.

Fear will keep you from serving the Lord. Especially if you fear what people think of you.

He gave talents to three different people, two of those people put their talents to usury and doubled them. But one knew that God was a righteous God a just God, so he buried his. He wanted it in a safe place. What was his fear? His fear was failure. His fear was losing. Do you fear failure? Do you fear losing? Why?

_____

_____

_____

_____

You know it's a wonderful time when you can trust God with your shortcomings (your fears), as well as with your greatness. In every one of your lives He has put great things. In every one of your lives there are things that you are not so great in. Can you trust Him with those?

Sometimes the pastor must tell people things that they don't want to hear. Sometimes they get angry. Sometimes they just put up with me. Sometimes they come back later and say the reason I am back pastor is because you told me the truth when everyone else told me the other. You see when you tell people what God said, you are telling them the truth. You cannot have a good relationship without truth and you cannot have a good relationship without faith. You must trust the Lord with those who do not like you.

_____

_____

_____

_____

In John 16:33 it says, "These things I have spoken unto you, that in me ye might have peace. In the world ye shall have tribulation: but be of good cheer; I have overcome the world."

_____

_____

_____

In I John 5:4 it says, "For whatsoever is born of God overcomes the world: and this is the victory that overcometh the world, even our faith." Jesus has overcome the world and He says your faith will overcome the world. Faith in Jesus helps us over anxiety, over sin, over boredom, depression, despair, death, discontent. What causes us not to have a sound mind? A lot of time it is anxiety, or depression.

_____

_____

_____

_____

Fear makes the wolf a giant. Faith makes the wolf small. He who fears death cannot enjoy life.

"Whosoever shall call upon the name of the Lord shall be saved." (Romans 10:13).

"But as many as received him, to them gave he power to become the sons of God." (John 1:12).

Session 14 - Four Types of Faith

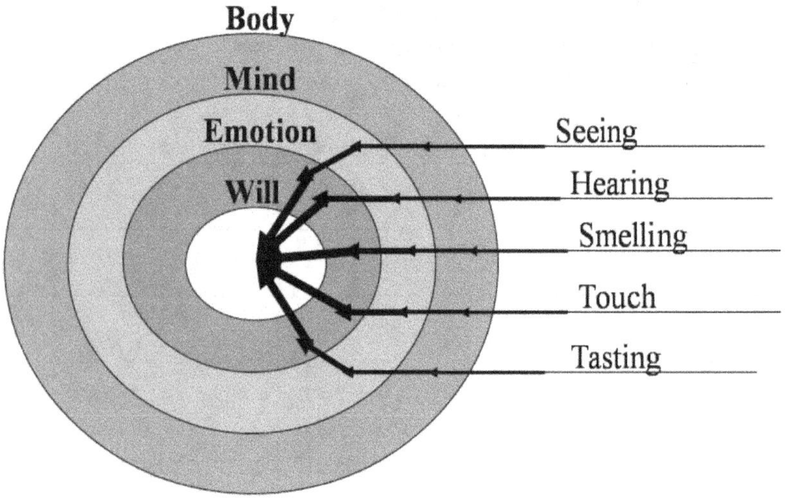

Body

Mind

Emotion —————— Seeing

Will —————— Hearing

—————— Smelling

—————— Touch

—————— Tasting

_____

_____

_____

_____

_____

_____

_____

_____

Four Kinds of Faith

1._____

_____

_____

_____

2._____

_____

_____

_____

3._____

_____

_____

_____

4._____

_____

_____

_____

Here is the key from John 1:12 "But as many as received him, to them gave the power to become the sons of God, even to them that believe on his name. The gift is not yours until you have received it."

_____

_____

_____

_____

Session 15 - What's Next ?

What's next in your journey in your marriage? Are you ready to let THE Marriage Builder help you? Can He take over your marriage and build it on the Solid Rock? He can, if you decide to let Him. Below with your spouse, I want you together to write out what is next on your journey together. How are your going to let THE Marriage Builder bless you in your journey?

I hope God has richly blessed you in these few days. Be sure to let the Light shine!

_____

_____

_____

_____

_____

_____

_____

_____

_____

_____

_____

_____

_____

_____

_____

Thank you for attending the Marriage Builders' Seminar. We hope that it has been a blessing to you. We hope that you will tell others about the seminar. You can check our website to schedule a workshop in your church. Be sure to check often. We also have the seminar on the website so that you can listen to it again. We hope that God will give you the ability to grow your marriage and to bless others with it.

Fireside Ministries

The Fireside Ministries was born from the vision that one man had to bring people together with Jesus through spiritual healing. Out of this, the Marriage Builders' Seminar was born to help guide people through spiritual healing through Jesus Christ.

Fireside Ministries is in Tiger, GA.

Marriage Builder Seminar

The Marriage Builder Seminar is a week-end long teaching that will help married couples, singles and those getting ready for marriage. If you would like to have a seminar at your Fellowship, please go to our web site at firesideministries2020@gmail.com and click on the seminar to get in contact with us.

 **Marriage Builder Seminar**

Marriage Builder Seminar

 **Marriage Builder Seminar**

 **Marriage Builder Seminar**

 **Marriage Builder Seminar**

 **Marriage Builder Seminar**

www.ingramcontent.com/pod-product-compliance
Lightning Source LLC
Chambersburg PA
CBHW081414280526
45788CB00009B/3096